F-15E Strike Eagle

Hans Halberstadt

Windrow & Greene

Published in Great Britain 1992 by
Windrow & Greene Ltd.
5 Gerrard Street
London W1V 7LJ

ISBN 1-872004-27-X

Published in the USA by
Speciality Press Publishers
& Wholesalers Inc.
PO Box 338
Stillwater, MN 55082
(612) 430-2210/800-888-9653

Acknowledgements
Although the author gets the credit, in
fact many people are really responsible for a book. In this case Lt. Col.
Steve Turner, commander of the 336th
Tactical Fighter Squadron, is as guilty
as anybody. His kind hospitality and
energetic support of the project were
the foundation of its success. Many
other 'Rocketeers' helped out; I would
especially like to salute Capt. Wayne
Gesellschap, 1st Lt. Brad Freels, 1st Lt.
Dan Holmes and 1st Lt. Ray Toth for
their time and attention.

F-15 drivers are trained at Luke AFB,
where the public affairs shop is
blessed with Mr. Bill McKenzie, who
knows all the angles. One of the
instructors, Capt. 'Bones' Dennee, provided much material for the captions
and narrative.

The Air Force's excellent public af-
fairs operation once again provided
superb assistance, thanks to Capt.
Kevin Baggett at Tactical Air Com-
mand, and Capt. Davis and Mr. Jay
Barber at Seymour Johnson AFB.
Hans Halberstadt
San Jose, California
November 1991

(Title page) They say the wing is as
big as a tennis court, and it feels that
way when you're wandering around
on it. The speed brake is visible
behind the canopy.

1: The Mighty 4th

At the End of Runway arming area, a Strike Eagle tests its wings. The crews call this the 'last chance' check area, where each jet is carefully inspected for flaws large and small, e.g leaks, loose panels, cracks, and the occasional loose missile. They find some, too.

August 1990. Summer evenings in North Carolina are warm and soft with moisture. The sun sets in a muted orange ball over the hangars and ramps where the F-15E Strike Eagles are parked. The first jets taxy out of the parking spaces and trundle down the ramp. Red flags flutter from the wings where safety pins still secure missiles to the underwing pylons. It's a mile from the parking area to the end of the runway and the Strike Eagles roll along quietly, one after another. Alongside the taxyway are armed guards and Air Force personnel in scattered clusters. They wave; some salute, others hold up signs.

Alongside the taxyway tonight, just like any other night, a crew measures the weight of each aircraft as it rolls up to the final arming point. They hold up a display with the exact weight for the pilot to record.

The Strike Eagles are heavy this evening, loaded down with tanks and Stinger and Sidewinder missiles. The take-off runs will be lengthy.

A hundred metres farther on the Strike Eagles park, side-by-side, and are attended to by a crew of ordnancemen. They chock the wheels, then swarm over each jet in turn, checking for leaks, loose fittings and panels, and finally pulling the pins that safe the weapons. The crew leader signals for the chocks to be pulled, then signals the pilot to move forward — he is ready for flight. As the aircraft starts to move the crewman comes to the position of attention, raising his right hand in a crisp salute. The pilot returns the salute, holds it for two seconds, and the Strike Eagle is on its way.

The flight is cleared onto the runway and they form

up, two at a time. As power is applied, the huge turbine engines turn fuel into noise and heat and power. The Strike Eagles start to roll. Afterburners kick in, consuming 40,000 lbs of fuel an hour, throwing a pointed blowtorch of flame thirty feet behind the fighter. A mile down the runway, at 185 knots, the main wheels leave the concrete and the Strike Eagles are airborne. Wheels up, flaps up, throttle back out of 'burner to Military Power. The F-15Es point their noses up, establish a 5,000 feet-per-minute rate of climb, and disappear into the gathering night.

Wingmen join on leaders. The flights form up and come left to an easterly course, levelling off at 25,000 feet. Below, through gaps in the cloud, in the last light of a summer evening, towns and farms slip astern at 350 knots calibrated airspeed, about 500 miles an hour.

The coastline appears, a thin strip of sand and white breakers on a grey ocean. Then the coast is gone, replaced by the dark Atlantic, and above is the deep blue vault of space.

An hour out of Seymour Johnson, a KC-10's navigation strobe and position lights appear ahead and above. The tanker will lead the flight across the ocean, a gas station in the sky — the tanker crews call it a 'fighter drag'. Back at the tail of the KC-10, the boom operator has opened the panel that protects his huge window on the world, the largest piece of pressurized glass in the United States Air Force. He runs his tests and the boom extends, waiting for the first customer.

The first Eagle darts quickly into view, slides below and into range of the long tube. The boom operator flies the boom toward the open receptacle on the jet's

The speed brake is effective, but not as effective as the big wing itself when it comes to stopping the jet on landing. Just the same, the crews want to make sure it works before rolling out onto the active runway.

A brace of Strike Eagles from the 4th
Tactical Wing taxy out from the
parking area for a little sport.

It's a long way to the runway if you want to rock and roll — a mile, in this case.

left wing. The F-15E squirms in the turbulence caused by the passage of the big tanker, looking like some exotic mechanical creature waiting to mate. The probe extends, couples, locks, and the delivery begins — 2,000 lbs of JP4 per minute. The Strike Eagle continues to wiggle, up and down, left and right, seemingly at risk of breaking off. At last, satisfied, it is uncoupled, and dances away out of the light. Another slides quickly up out of the gloom to take its place.

The parade of Eagles and the big tanker will fly this way through the night, across the ocean, around to the other side of the world. They are part of the vanguard sent to oppose Iraq, to defend Saudi Arabia and the other nations of the Persian Gulf, and they are expecting to fight. That's how the Strike Eagle went to war in August of 1990. It would be another five months before the shooting began, and before the Strike Eagle became one of the great success stories of the war.

The F-15E Strike Eagle is a marvelous aircraft, a combat-proven design that serves as the United States' premier fighter-bomber. It is a design that is actually older than most of its pilots, yet it is also full of leading edge technologies. It is $44 million worth of aluminum, composites, black boxes, plexiglass, microprocessors, wiring and hydraulics: 63 feet long, 18 feet high, 40 feet across; about 40,000 lbs dry and bare, 81,000 lbs at max take off weight. It will fly and fight as fast as Mach 2.5 or as slow as 200 knots. The Strike Eagle will kill a MiG sixty miles away, over the horizon, or put a laser-guided bomb through the front door of a bunker full of ammunition. It will shoot any missile, drop any bomb that the USAF owns, including the nukes, Sparrows and Sidewinders, Mavericks, Paveways, Rockeyes, HARMs and Harpoons. The Strike Eagle carries a 20 mm gun for those nasty, close-in furballs, and for the occasional ground target. It will

pull nine negative Gs and more, but the pilots can't. It will push three positive Gs, although the pilots hate every one. An early model stuck its nose in the air and kept going to 102,000 feet, setting a time-to-altitude record in the process. It's good high, good low, day or night, near or far, against bad guys in the air or on the ground. No wonder they call it the Dual Role fighter.

The Strike Eagle went to war a week after Iraq invaded Kuwait. The 336th Tactical Fighter Squadron (TFS), a component of the 4th TFW, was the first interdiction unit to deploy. There were just 24 Strike Eagles in those first days, guarding Saudi Arabian ports, airfields, and cities against an invasion that never came, providing air cover for the build-up that came with a vengeance.

The shooting started on 16 January 1991 at 2100 hours Washington time. When it finally stopped six weeks later the 336th TFS 'Rocketeers' had flown 1088 combat missions totalling 3274 combat hours, hitting bridges, tanks, troop concentrations, artillery batteries, and every enemy missile launcher they could find. They spent six million pounds of bombs and missiles. They spent three good airframes, one in training and two in combat; and they lost four good aviators killed and four captured.

A new squadron, the 335th TFS 'Chiefs', was despatched in October of 1990 and joined the 336th. The 335th flew more than 1200 missions, totalling more than 4000 combat hours. They killed 45 enemy aircraft on the ground, 23 communications facilities, 36 bridges, 478 armoured vehicles, and 48 SCUD missiles. One Strike Eagle from the 335th made history on 14 February when it attacked a helicopter in flight with a laser-guided bomb, scoring a kill.

9

It's hard to believe, but this elegant, exotic airframe goes back 30 years — longer than many of its pilots. Lt. Col. Steve Turner, commander of the 336th Tactical Fighter Squadron, taxies out for a night flight training mission.

All buttoned up, an F-15 works through the 'before taxi' checklist.

Ahead of a gathering summer storm, a Strike Eagle heads out of the parking area.

The 4th Tactical Wing commander's jet is easily identified by the big block letters with the white outline on the rudders. This was the first Strike Eagle delivered to an operational squadron.

It's a *big* airplane. Ready to start engines, the Strike Eagle dwarfs its crew chief.

'Are you sure the air conditioning is set to EMERGENCY?' The greenhouse effect in a fighter cockpit is severe, and the canopy does not come down until the engines are started and the cold air is blasting out of the vents.

All F-15 take-offs are done with the throttle full forward in afterburner.

The two-ship formation is standard in the United States Air Force: a leader and a wingman. For most of the mission very little communication between aircraft takes place — the wingman sticks to the leader, does what he does and follows the standard operating procedure. The SOP is customised in the briefing that precedes every flight. In combat, the leader and the wingman will often fly a line-abreast formation, about a mile between them. Each guards against air-to-air threats in his own sector.
(*Randy Jolly photograph*)

The Strike Eagle is $44 million worth of black boxes, composites, aluminum, computers, hydraulics, and some rather inspired design work. The E-model of the F-15 is readily identified in flight by its two-seat cockpit and darker paint scheme. (*Randy Jolly photograph*)

Squirming into position behind a KC-10 tanker, a Seymour Johnson-based Eagle is buffeted by the wake of the big airframe. (*Randy Jolly photograph*)

When head-on, the Strike Eagle's portly waistline is clearly visible, the bulging air intake fairings containing 4,875 lbs of fuel in each conformal fuel tank (CFT). Unlike normal external tanks the CFTs on the F-15E have the capacity to carry ordnance mounted on special weapons racks; these devices create virtually no drag at either sub- or supersonic speeds, and are fully G-rated. (*USAF photograph*)

Satisfied for the moment, a freshly
serviced Eagle drops astern and
clears the tanker. Eagles consume
prodigious amounts of fuel and need
to be fed regularly — about every
hour and a half. In combat, with the
afterburner lit and down in the weeds,
the jet sucks up about 90,000 lbs of
fuel an hour; for ferry flights,
throttled back, it's more like 20,000
pounds.
(*Randy Jolly photograph*)

2: Flying The Eagle

'Cheated death again!' is the old saying: two young members of the 336th TFS return from a training flight.

The last thing most crews do before mounting their semi-trusty steed is to clip and adjust the buckles on the parachute harness. To be worn properly the harness needs to be snug — too snug to walk comfortably, so it is left loose until the last minute. The parachute is part of the ejection seat system, so the pilot's harness is attached to the seat with large quick-release buckles as part of the pre-start procedures. The harness goes over the survival vest, with its radio, mirror, flares, smoke, food and water and, for a combat mission, a pistol. In the seat itself is a raft, more survival supplies, and an oxygen bottle for those dreaded high altitude ejections. As remote as the possibility of a catastrophic problem in flight might appear, most squadrons have pilots who've had to abandon aircraft in flight, some of them more than once.

lying any kind of aeroplane, from a little rag-wing to a grand 747, is kind of a ritual activity, a sort of ceremony, a performance, like meeting the Queen or receiving an Oscar. Flying a fighter is especially like that. You must dress properly for the occasion; there are proper manners to be observed; you are judged by what you say, how you say it, what you do and how you do it. Formally and informally your friends and accomplices will rate you, fit you into the list of better and worse. Even with aircraft, even with the Strike Eagle, there are artists and hacks, and journeymen pilots, too.

You don't wear a white tie and tails but a Nomex flight suit, with cotton underwear and heavy boots. Nomex doesn't melt or burn when the jet catches fire — a small but important factor if you happen to be sitting in a smouldering warplane. You'll need Nomex gloves, too, and a skull cap of the same material to wear under your helmet, all of which provide that extra margin of protection against fire. The guys in Life Support store your gear and maintain it — the harness for the parachute that stays with the aircraft; the survival vest with its many little bits and pieces (fish hooks, knife, water bottle, flashlight, strobe, smoke marker, pencil flare gun, pistol and ammunition, signal mirror, rescue radio). They will custom-fit your helmet for you, and your oxygen mask too, and make sure that they are kept clean, undamaged, and ready just for you. They will fit a set of 'speed jeans' for you too, the pneumatic chaps that fit over your lower abdomen and legs and inflate during high-G manoeuvres to help prevent black-out. It all goes in your personal locker until you're ready to fly.

A couple of hours before flight time you gather in a briefing room with the other crews. The mission is outlined in a standard format: objectives, start and taxy times, call signs, routes, altitudes, frequencies, IFF squawk codes . . . write it down. Then, an hour or so before take-off, it is time to 'step'.

The crew chief will have done a thorough preflight inspection; but he's not taking it skyward, you are. Give it a walkaround inspection, starting at the boarding ladder and working around clockwise, following the checklist in the Dash One. Look for anything loose, broken, bent, abraded, burned, missing. Then up the ladder and inspect the upper surface of the wing, control surfaces, inlets, and speed brake. Okay, get in.

Your Place of Business

From the left intake, with one hand on the canopy bow, swing a leg over the rail and pour yourself into the front seat. In front, at eye-level, is the biggest, widest HUD in the Air Force. The size has many advantages, particularly at night when the only image of the outside world you have is a thermal or radar display projected on it. During the day the HUD displays airspeed, attitude, angle of attack, dive angle, altitude, missile priority status including range to target and in or out of parameters. The HUD has several master modes, each offering a set of data on the display, air-to-air, air-to-ground, instrument, etc. Select air-to-ground and the HUD displays the gun pipper for you.

Below the HUD, covering most of the front panel, are four cathode ray tube displays (CRT), three colour and one monochrome. There are 16 different displays possible for these screens at the command of the pilot. There's air-to-air radar, air-to-ground radar, forward looking infrared (FLIR), horizontal situation indicator, attitude indicator, HUD repeater, FACTS page that lists all your available weapons and how they'll come off,

Two crews amble out to their aircraft. Despite the popular notion of fighter crews being baby-faced post-adolescents, most are in their thirties, and the best ones are sometimes the elderly majors and lieutenant-colonels in their forties. In fighters, as elsewhere, experience counts.

Well, look at that — both engines are still there! The walkaround inspection looks casual, but for the guys who trust their lives to the machine it is a last opportunity to catch a problem before it becomes life-threatening. And they do catch them.

A back-seater takes a final look around before climbing into the 'pit' and spending another hour and a half keeping his buddy up front from becoming totally lost.

(Right) You can't do anything with government property without paperwork. The crew chief reviews the Form 781 with the pilot — there are almost always minor problems with an aircraft that don't interfere with safe flight, but need to be considered.

(Right below) The squadron commander, Lt.Col. Steve Turner, and his back-seater check the 781 before climbing up to the cockpit.

plus the tactical situation display — a moving map with an image of the aeroplane superimposed on your current position.

The Strike Eagle's cockpit seems almost barren by comparison with earlier aircraft, many of the old analog instruments being replaced by the CRTs. This doesn't make the pilot's workload any lighter, though — he just gets more to do.

The heart of all this elegance is a panel called the 'up-front controller', a kind of key pad with a few lines for data display. This one little panel is used to programme all the subsystems that need to be fed information — the inertial navigation system, the radios, the TACAN, and more. It can handle four radios, the TACAN, the instrument landing system, IFF transponder, air-to-air interrogation and INS waypoints. It displays data pages — like how much fuel remains, how long to the next waypoint, and lots more. You can also correct weapons delivery errors, and control the secure radios as well as the HAVE QUICK system.

The cockpit is also designed around the HOTAS concept of 'hands-on-throttle-and-stick'. It used to be that a pilot had to let go of one of the controls when he wanted to arm a missile, change a frequency, or manage any of the dozens of other cockpit chores required in flight. In combat, where G-forces often make any kind of movement nearly impossible, this can create quite a problem. So the throttle and the stick are studded with buttons that let the pilot make the

critical changes with just the press of a finger. Combined with the HUD and the tremendous performance of the airframe/engine design, this means that an F-15E Strike Eagle pilot can manoeuvre at high G loads and retain situational awareness and control in ways his enemy probably cannot duplicate. There are good threat airframes out there, and there are good threat pilots out there too, but the Strike Eagle pilot expects to win against them every time because of the way that he assimilates with his jet.

The throttles have controls to select missiles or gun, to designate/undesignate a target, operate the speed brake, radio and radar controls, cursor control for target selection, the laser rangefinder, chaff and flare dispenser, a button for missile boresight and air-to-air interrogation.

The stick grip has a castle-shaped thumb switch that controls the individual CRT screens, and the data that's been programmed for each. There are standard 'pickle' button and trigger switches, and a trim button on top of the grip. The trim button doubles as a countermeasures dispenser when it is pressed down. Another switch will undesignate a target on the air-to-air radar and operate several other auto-acquisition functions of the radar targeting system. This mode lets the radar lock onto the first bogey that comes in range and in parameters which the pilot or EWO programmes into the system, and sets up the weapons for a shot. The EWO or the pilot have to decide if it's a good shot to take, but the system at least sets up against what it expects to be the highest priority victim.

Another feature of the cockpit is a computer-synthesized voice driven by one of the many black boxes, a strange, female voice the crews refer to as 'Bitching Betty'. She warns of overtemps in the engines, or fires,

or low altitude, or almost anything else that puts the Eagle at risk. The voice is crabby and loud, and is one of the few things in the cockpit that can't be adjusted. The crews don't like her, but they understand her good intentions. They hear from her often, especially in combat.

Well, as long as you're in the cockpit you might as well take it for a ride. The start sequence is extremely simple: no key, no battery, no external power required. A jet fuel starter (JFS) control on the right side of the cockpit will get you in business using hydraulic pressure in an accumulator. Generator switch for the right engine to ON, JFS handle pulled, and a green ready light illuminates. Right engine is lit first; so advance the right throttle just past the detent ('over the horn', they say). The JFS spools up the engine, and the fuel control system and ignition sequence performs automatically. At 50 per cent RPM the JFS disengages, the generators start putting out juice, the hydraulic system starts performing and the JFS is recharged in seconds. Then the left engine is started in the same way.

With the engines started, use the built-in tests to check the flight controls (which takes about four or five minutes), the radar, air flow, and other systems. You can be good to go in about ten minutes, most of which is required to initialize the Inertial Navigation System.

The crew chief will then pull the mike cord he's used to talk to you during run-up. You call for taxy clearance, and then you're signalled out of the parking spot, a crisp salute sending you off down the taxyway. Steer with the rudder pedals; they are coupled to the nose wheel at low speeds. You motor along at about 15 to 20 mph, and try to keep it on the centreline — beginners tend to wander a bit.

Out at the arming area near the end of the runway,

The emblem of the 336th Tactical Fighter Squadron, nicknamed the 'Rocketeers'.

1st Lt. Ray 'Chip' Toth, Weapons System Officer. The Strike Eagle is the premier assignment for a young Air Force officer coming out of Undergraduate Pilot Training (UPT), so it goes only to the most accomplished. 1st Lt. Toth earned his seat in the jet with a degree in aerospace engineering from Penn State — he came first in his UPT navigator school. He's got 115 hours in the E, 230 hours total time. In the ancient tradition of Air Force nicknames, somebody decided that Toth sounded like 'tooth' and that inspired the name, even without any chips.

1st Lt. Dan 'Bop' Holmes, Pilot. Also first in his UPT class, and with a similar degree, 1st Lt. Holmes took a degree in Aeronautical Operations from San Jose State University in California. When this photo was taken he had 140 hours in the E, and 450 hours in all types. He, like his partner, has been in the Air Force for three years. Both are very junior pilots in a squadron loaded with senior captains, majors, and lieutenant-colonels. Both have to say 'sir' to just about everybody.

Clear visor in place for a flight that will go on into darkness, Lt. Holmes is ready to close the canopy and get down to business.

park again for a quick 'last chance' check. The jet is thoroughly inspected for leaks, loose components and anything else that might cause problems in flight. When the pins are pulled from the missiles and bombs they are armed, so be careful with those buttons.

With a take-off clearance from the tower, roll on out, line up on the runway centreline and hold in position. There is about two miles of concrete in front of you, most of which you should not need. Run the engines up to 80 per cent — you should see engine temperatures of about 600 degrees centigrade, 4,000 lbs of fuel flow and about 20 on the engine nozzle position indicator. If everything is close, release the toe-brakes and smoothly apply power up through 'Military Power' and into 'burner. The acceleration is like that experienced in a moderately good sports car, except it doesn't stop. The first go/no-go speed is 100 knots — if you have a tyre blow before, stop the aircraft — after that you need to get airborne and sort it out later.

At 140 knots bring the stick back about half way to your lap and the nose will lift from the runway. When the HUD shows your angle of attack at about 10 to 13 degrees, hold it there by easing the stick forward. The jet will come off the ground all by itself at about 160 knots if it's light, about 185 knots if it's heavy. You'll use about 1,500 feet of runway for a light jet, 5,000 if you're heavy.

Get the gear up as soon as you've got a positive rate of climb, no later than 250 knots. Then the flaps come up and set up a good rate of climb — 330 to 350 knots airspeed will give you a nice, conservative 5,000-feet-per-minute. The jet will climb out much faster, but if you're sorting out a formation this makes it easier for everybody to catch up and slide into place.

As you throttle back from 'burner to 'Mil Power' the engines are no longer gulping fuel at the rate of 90,000 lbs per hour but only using about 20,000. Level off at your assigned altitude, preferably somewhere around 22,000 feet — fuel economy improves with altitude. Coming back from Baghdad, Strike Eagles liked to get up to 40,000 for the hour commute back to the barn. Up at that altitude the airspeed indicator will read only about 300 knots, but your ground speed will be around 500 to 600.

Okay, it's time to put this thing back on the ground. Normal approach for a two-ship mission varies from one command to another. A typical one has the aircraft flying abreast, about a mile apart; both 'break' into the pattern simultaneously, resulting in a trail formation with about 5000 feet separation. Throttle back to maintain about 250 knots airspeed or as required to avoid overrunning the leader; gear down, flaps down, maintain the pattern altitude — about 1700 AGL on the down wind leg. With the touch down point at your eight o'clock position, turn base. The wing tip will point at the runway as you make a smooth, descending turn to the centreline. You come out of the turn lined up on the runway, nose down about ten degrees, about a mile from the numbers and with about 300 above the

ground. The ground will start to rush up at you, and the centreline and numbers should be centered in the HUD. Power adjustments will keep you on the glide slope. The HUD will show about 160 knots calibrated airspeed, about 130 knots on the ground. The wheels will touch and if you hold the nose up the big wing will quickly slow the jet down to 90 knots. If the flaps come up you can 'aero-brake' longer. The speed brake works, but not as well as the wing.

The Back Seat

The rear cockpit is very similar to the front, with a few exceptions. There is no HUD, but the HUD information can be displayed on one of the CRTs. The EWO can and does fly the aircraft and can do almost everything the front-seater can do, including land. He can't fire air-to-air missiles, shoot the gun, or lower the flaps, however. If the back-seater has to lower the gear it is an emergency procedure. He has four CRTs, two colour and

Lieutenants Toth and Holmes perform the mission as a single crew; 'the front-seater rows the boat, the back-seater shoots the ducks', is the way they explain it. The F-15 Strike Eagle's mission is far too much work for one man (even with the help of a computer) to cope with, and it is a lot of work for two.

two monochrome, and two hand controllers on each side of the cockpit that allow the same HOTAS functions as in the front cockpit.

The EWO's primary job is to manage the radar. While the front-seater keeps the aircraft airborne and pointed in the right direction, maintains position relative to the other aircraft in the flight, and keeps alert for bogeys, the EWO keeps busy looking for threats and targets. Both spend a lot of time using the old reliable 'Mk One Eyeball', watching outside for hazards or opportunities. Since the primary mission of the Strike Eagle is air-to-ground, and since this is most safely performed under the cloak of darkness, the EWO becomes an artist with the radar mapping function of the Eagle and the targeting pod of the LANTIRN. Unless a bogey gets within ten miles, the pilot doesn't usually mess with the radar. The EWO backs up the front-seater on navigation, systems update, the threat radar warning receiver, and other chores.

Radar mapping requires that the jet be flown off to the side of the target area. It is 'painted' by the radar, which results in a detailed monochrome picture that can be used to designate weapons delivery.

'What makes this airplane so unique is its cockpit design, its human machine interface is more advanced than I've seen in any other type. It had to be that way because the airplane can do so much; otherwise it would just be overwhelming! It seems overwhelming at first, but it soon becomes second nature.

'It is an incredible airplane! Being able to fly low level, at night, doing an air-to-air sweep while performing an air-to-ground mission at the same time is very easy. Can anybody else do the mission? The F-16 has LANTIRN, but it doesn't have that reach-out-and-touch-somebody capability while we have the AIM-7. It may be theoretically possible for a single-seat aircraft like the F-16 to perform our missions, but I think you'd lose a lot of guys if you tried doing that.

The face of experience. The historical 336th TFS badge is worn with pride by all aircrew, 'velcro'd' onto the right shoulder of the overall.

'We don't have a lot of the stealth technology that the F-117 or the YF-22 have, but we have much more advanced technology than the F-117 that lets us go in at low level. It is very much a crew cockpit. The back-seater is responsible for getting at least 50 per cent of the mission done. You couldn't get the job done without him.'

Mission Recalled

'We trained to do the low-level deep interdiction attack mission in a heavy threat environment, but I only flew one mission like that in *Desert Storm*, my first mission on the first night of the war. We went in at 300 feet to drop five Mk 84s on a bridge. We went in low, popped up to drop the bombs, and went back down to go home.

'After that first night the threat degraded so much that the rest of the missions were flown at higher altitudes. They were shooting SAMs but apparently without guidance, just to get us to drop our ordnance, and it worked at first until we caught on. It was kind of smart of them, in a way, because they were successful in defeating the mission of those guys who thought they were being guided on.

'Typically, we'd go up high to avoid the triple-A, approach the target until about 30 miles out, then we'd

(Left and above) It's hard to look cute wearing one of these things the way they have to be worn, so Tom Cruise always let his dangle in the film 'Top Gun'. But when it comes time to punch out, or something else goes wrong, you don't have time — or enough hands — to start putting it on. It goes on early and stays on for the whole flight. Properly fitted, it is tight; breathing with it must be learned. But when the pressurization system fails (and they do) at 40,000 feet, an aviator has seconds to recognize the problem and do something about it.

Nobody flies in an F-15 without the little orange 'chamber card' that is issued to graduates of the aviation physiology course. The bulk of the programme deals with the effects of hypoxia — oxygen deprivation. It is a problem that kills aircrew every year, in strange and sometimes subtle ways. Often the only clue will be slurred speech, difficulty concentrating, giddiness, tunnel vision, or fatigue. By the time hypoxia is noticed one of the most difficult and challenging manoeuvres a pilot or 'wizzo' can face is to force his left hand over to the Oxygen Regulator Control panel and push all three switches up, to ON, FULL, and EMERGENCY. The mask is just one part of a system of life support equipment designed for a dangerous environment. And the mask, along with the visor, protects the crewman from smoke in the cockpit, or from the 500 mph blast of wind in an ejection.

CAPT GREG HASTY
CAPT JOHN AYMONIN

There's a lot of waiting involved in fighter operations. This crew is waiting for the rest of the flight to get the 'last chance' check and have their weapons armed.

'check away', fly off at about 45 degrees so the radar could map the target. The back-seater would find the target, designate, take the radar map down to a .67 (a detailed picture of an area about 3,000 feet on a side). The radar produces a black and white image of the target, with gun emplacements or SAMs or whatever clearly visible, and you just mark your chosen target with the cursor and push a button to designate it.

'The computer figures out a solution, feeds it to the HUD, and all the pilot has to do at this point is line up the steering. At about six or seven miles we'd start a diving delivery, using the FLIR to find the target. If the designation was good a little diamond symbol would appear on it. I'd pull up, using the HUD symbology for guidance. The computer gives you an azimuth steer line — you line up on that and the velocity vector indicator — and at about six or seven miles we roll inverted, nose down about 30 degrees, and you should be able to see the target. Now, check the designation; it should be good — if not, designate again. Hold down the 'pickle switch' that provides consent to the computer and fly to the HUD symbology. The bombs will come off without any further attention, and should land on the target.

'My most memorable mission was my first. I was more scared on that one! I was number two, dropping Mk 84 bombs on a bridge. We were each dropping five, and the Mk 84 is a *big* bomb and five is a lot of ordnance. Well, my lead was a little out of position when the bombs came off, with the result that all the bombs hit at the same time. It was the biggest explosion I have ever seen, and combined with the darkness, the tension of the first mission and the first day of the war, this made it a very memorable occasion.

'We attacked ammo dumps a couple of times, and when you hit one of those things it was like a Fourth of

All buttoned up in air-conditioned comfort, a crew is ready to taxy. The wide field holographic display's big green eye is easier to see through when viewed from inside the cockpit.

'Okay, sir, you're good-to-go!' The crisp salute from the crew chief is the traditional last signal to the aircraft commander telling him that he's ready for the skies.

(Right) 'Right turn' signals the crew chief as he moves the jet out of the blocks and onto the taxyway. At low speeds the pilot steers with the nose-wheel and differential braking. The crew chief does his best to ensure that the pilot avoids rubbing wingtips with adjacent aircraft or ground handling equipment.

Starting Two! One of the ground crew carefully inspects the left engine during the start sequence for any evidence of fire, leaks, or loose engine parts flying out the tail pipe.

July fireworks display. It would continue for hours! There was one dump that probably had 60 different bunkers. It was like 'The Price is Right', . . . which door are you going to take? So you'd map it, take one that looked like it hadn't been hit before, and bomb it. It would either be a dud or it would start putting out fireworks. The secondaries were really quite a kick. Some of the least pleasant memories I have are of the eight-and nine-hour sorties on the tanker doing SCUD hunts. It wasn't a lot of fun.

'We worked with JSTARS a lot and that was very satisfying. They could watch anything that moved on the ground or in the air. We used them exclusively in the Kuwaiti theatre. It was something new in warfare: real-time tasking. Aircraft were coming into an area every ten minutes loaded with bombs, and JSTARS would call you and say 'There's a troop concentration at so-and-so position', and you'd go and there they'd be and we'd bomb them. I got to feeling sorry for the poor bastards. At night you could see bombs going off everywhere, they were getting bombed all the time. It didn't surprise me in the least when the ground guys walked right through. There was nothing left.'

The enlisted crewmen who maintain the aircraft are often highly possessive of their Strike Eagles. They often say that they own the airframes and only loan them to the pilots to use — and they better be in good shape when they come back. It is a difficult job: hot in summer, freezing in winter, long hours — and they never get a ride. But the enlisted maintainers generally love the E model, and are rightly proud of their role in its success in *Desert Storm*.

The 4th TW's nest of Strike Eagles lined up nice and neat. Air Force aircraft introduce themselves with information on their tails — SJ for Seymour Johnson Air Force Base, North Carolina; AF for Air Force; 88 for the year of manufacture; and 1695 is the serial number for this airframe.

Before flight the jet gets a careful inspection for any foreign object that might somehow damage the aircraft, for any broken or loose or cracked or abraded component. Special overshoes are worn on the top of the jet to avoid damage from boots.

3: Walkaround

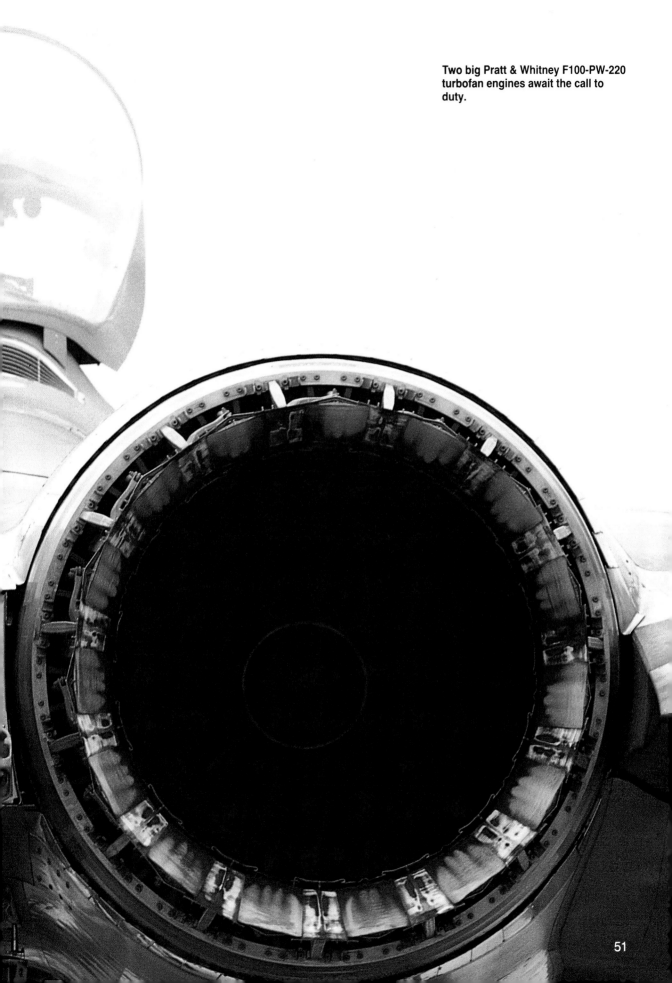

Two big Pratt & Whitney F100-PW-220 turbofan engines await the call to duty.

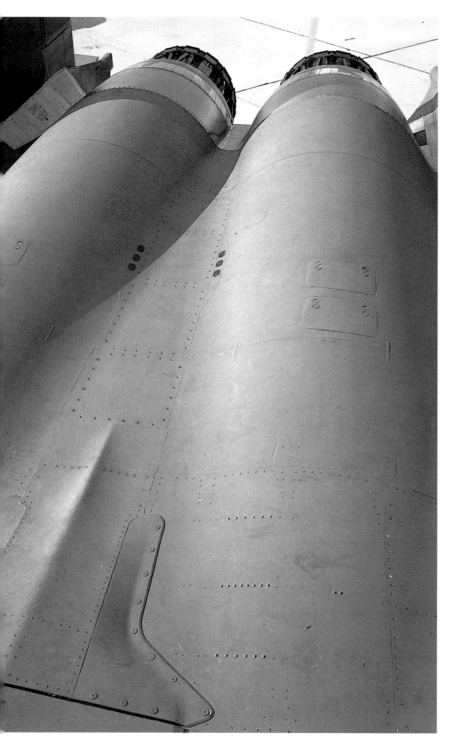

McDonnell Douglas completely revamped the engine bay area on the F-15E, although it still looks identical to that fitted to the F-15A/C; the difference lies mainly in the materials used for the engine bay covers. McDonnell Douglas pioneered the use of SPF/DB (superplastic formed and diffusion bonded) titanium. This high-tech material allows engineers to manufacture the covers as one large piece, rather than a series of smaller plates, due to its superb shaping qualities.

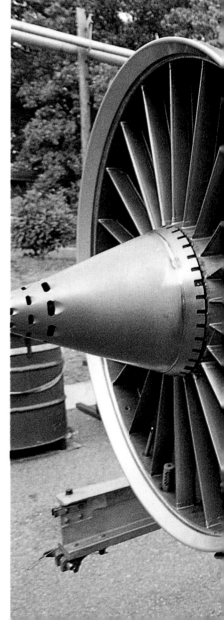

Pulled from a new aircraft for an acceptance inspection, a Pratt & Whitney F100-PW-220 waits to be towed to the engine shop where its nooks and crannies will be explored for cracks, loose bits, missing pieces, evidence of over-heats and anything else that the government would rather not pay for. The engine is the low-bypass 'leaky turbojet' type, an efficient converter of fossil fuels to noise, heat, and 24,000 lbs of thrust. It has proven a reliable, powerful, responsive powerplant, the foundation for the Strike Eagle's agility and speed.

(Right) The bombs proclaim a combat veteran, although not one with many missions. Although the pilots and 'wizzos' all have their names on an aircraft, they don't always get to fly them. When it comes time to fly, you take the jet that's available.

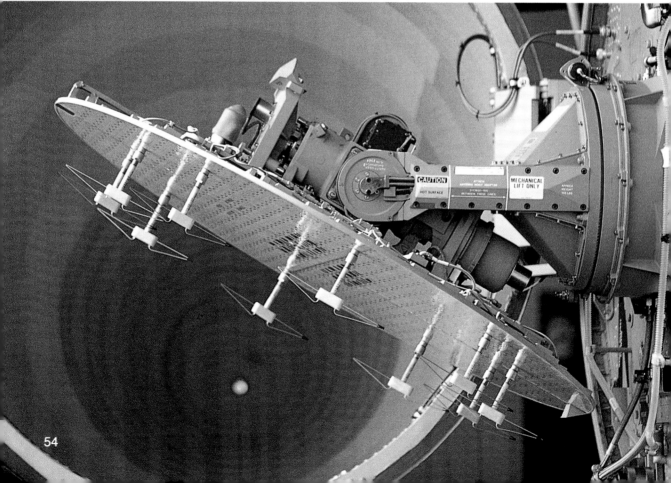

(Left) The Hughes APG-70 synthetic aperture radar. The system can be used to search for targets in the air, at ranges exceeding 40 miles, or can scan the ground to paint a highly detailed map that can be used to designate bombs.

(Left below) The radar antenna both transmits and receives, guides missiles, and puts out enough microwave energy to roast a turkey in fifteen seconds, if the turkey gets into the beam. Radars, consequently, can't be energized on the ground.

Another of the gee-whiz imaging systems is the Forward Looking Infrared (FLIR) part of the Low Altitude Navigation and Targeting Infrared for Night (LANTIRN) fire control system from Martin Marietta. This is the sensor head from the navigation pod — it 'sees' a thermal image of the terrain ahead of the aircraft in great detail, which can be viewed by the pilot and 'wizzo' on the HUD or on one of the multi-purpose display screens in the cockpits.

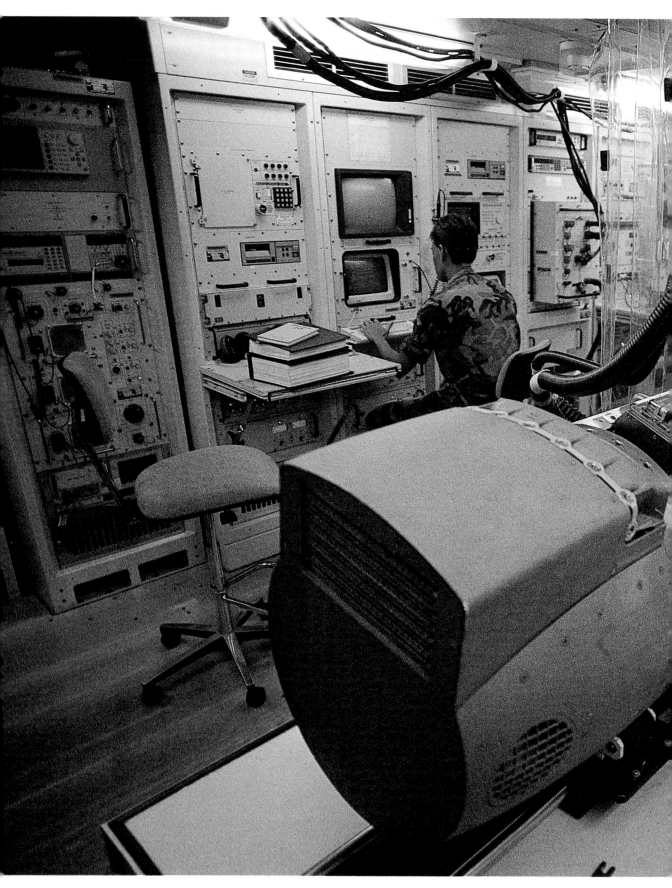

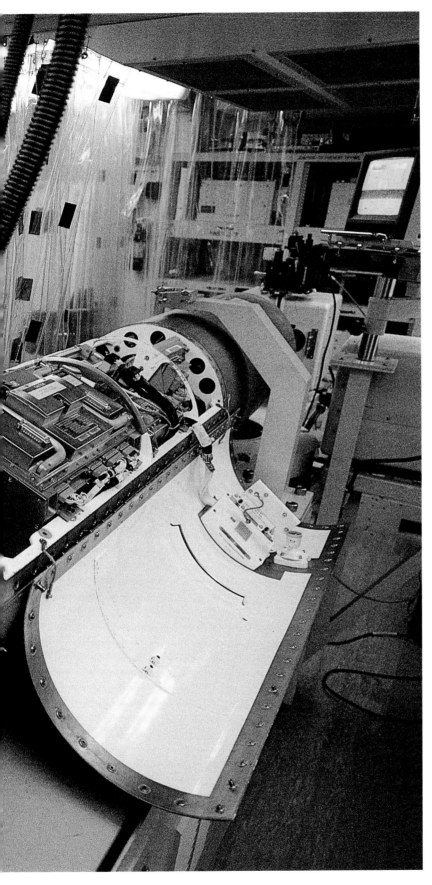

The LANTIRN pods are serviced in air-conditioned vans, away from the aircraft. There are two pods like this, mounted on inboard wing stations. The right pod is the Nav system, while the one on the left does the targeting. The Nav pod has its own terrain-following radar as well as the wide field FLIR, and together they've given USAF crews the capability to execute precision low-level attacks under the partial cover of darkness. The targeting pod has a separate FLIR and a laser rangefinder/designator, automatic target tracker, and automatic Maverick missile hand-off. The technicians who service these systems became extremely popular during *Desert Storm*. Not only did the pods work wonders — the air conditioned shelters needed to service them were the only refuges from the oppressive Arabian heat.

1st Lt. Dan Holmes ready for a night training mission.

SSGT E. MAYNES
SGT DAVID SILAGY

59

If you think this looks complicated, you should have seen the old C-model. Nearly everything the pilot needs to do can be done without looking inside the cockpit. When he does need to look at something it is probably on one of the three screens that dominate the panel, and the information is there because the 'wizzo' puts it there for him. There are two monochrome (green and black) screens and one colour up front, plus an engine monitor display. But when it comes time to leave in a hurry, the pilot probably won't have to look to find the ejection seat handles, even if they are painted bright yellow. Then it's sit up straight, head back against the rest, both hands on the seat handles, feet back full aft (if possible), grab *BOTH* handles and pull! The seat will get you clear and under a 'chute at 40,000 feet or even if the jet is parked on the ramp; but the odds are good that you'll be injured in the process, no matter what. Ejection is possible at airspeeds from zero to 600 knots, and beyond. Anything over 450 knots is going to get you hurt, and anything over 600 knots is going to hurt badly.

The information on each screen can be selected easily from a long menu. The panel between the two large monochrome screens is called the up-front controls: ten function buttons, six displays of 20 characters each, four radio controls, a 20 key data input section, and a brightness control. If that seems a lot, remember that it replaces many more controls that used to be dedicated to individual instruments and radios, reducing cockpit clutter tremendously. The small colour screen in front of the stick shows a moving map with the aircraft's position centred. This presentation — the Tactical Situation Display (TSD) — is coupled to the inertial navigation system (INS), an extremely accurate way of knowing where you are. Besides current position, the TSD also shows planned course, targets, aim points, and more. The map itself comes from a very low-tech piece of software — a 35 mm filmstrip that is loaded into a reader in the aft cockpit.

At the press of a button we now have an image from the FLIR on the monochrome displays and an artificial horizon on the colour multifunction screen. A built-in test menu is superimposed on the right screen.

Well, not much happening on the HUD, but tune in later for the latest hits. This is the 'plain vanilla' display, with aircraft heading, air speed, attitude, and not much more. But in flight the FLIR image can be displayed here, along with all the cues and symbology required to fly fast and low, to shoot guns and missiles, to drop bombs on targets, and to live to tell the tale.

'What do you mean, this isn't a full service station?' A pilot negotiates with ground crew before starting engines.

The control column in the front cockpit has eight switches and buttons, some with several functions. The round one at the far top will adjust the aircraft trim if it is displaced left/right or up/down, but if it is pushed in it will dispense flares or chaff; try not to get the functions confused, particularly if people are watching. The castle switch will cycle the displays or steer the FLIR sensor. The trigger has two positions; the first turns on the video gun camera, the second position fires the 20 mm gun. A button low on the grip, just right for the pinkie finger, will deactivate nosewheel steering on the ground or provide weapons control in the air. Below that is a paddle switch that can disengage the autopilot and can override the terrain following feature. The grip is attached to a force transducer that allows the aircraft to be flown even if the normal flight control system fails.

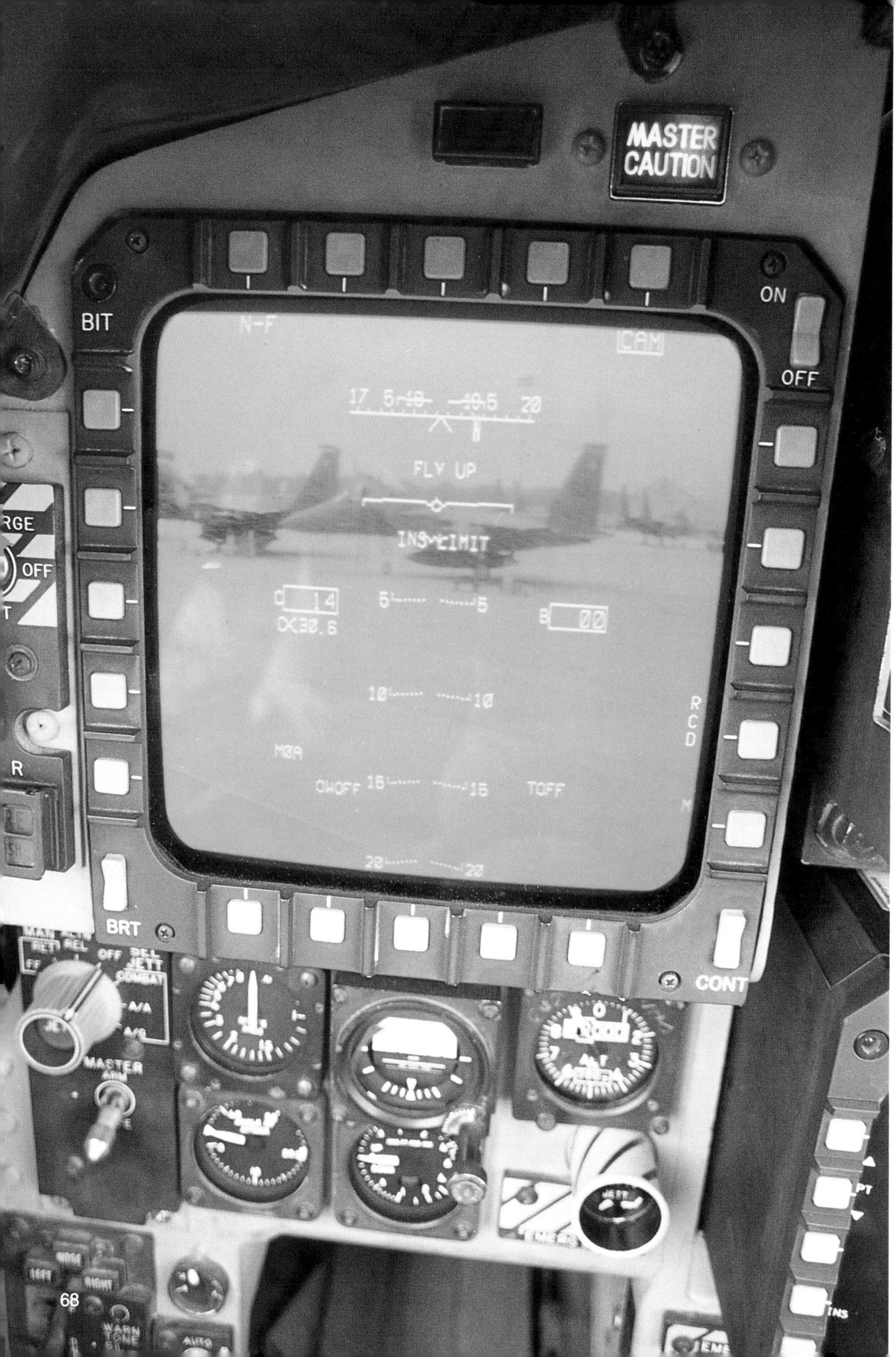
MASTER CAUTION
BIT
ON
OFF
N-F
CAM
FLY UP
INS LIMIT
BRT
CONT

(Left) One of the 'wizzo's' four displays; this one has the FLIR navigation pod's image combined with the HUD symbology. The 20 buttons around the screen are normally coupled to menu choices that are appropriate to each individual display.

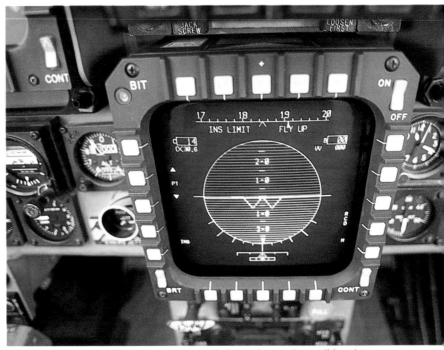

(Below) The 'wizzo' gets more of almost everything in the Strike Eagle, including two hand control grips and a throttle, too. The throttle has ten buttons, the control grip almost as many. Until you've actually tried to do something useful while pulling seven or eight Gs you have no idea what hard work can be; the hand controllers enable the pilot or 'wizzo' to designate targets, steer the FLIR or radar, select displays, fire guns or missiles, and all the other tactical chores that once had to wait until you eased off on the turn.

This very artificial horizon can be displayed on any of the scopes, and is quite handy for those instrument approaches on dark and stormy nights. It provides the same information as the traditional type, although you don't have to cage it, and it doesn't spin around idiotically when turned on like the ones in conventional instrument panels.

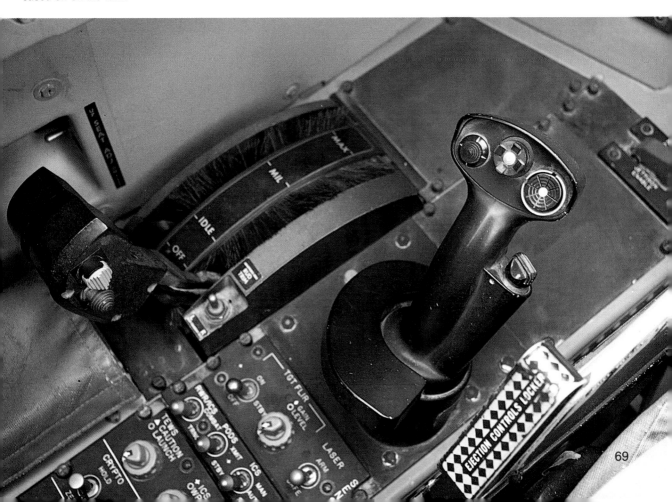

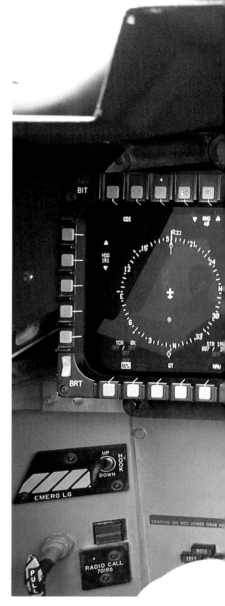

The 'wizzo's' up-front controller is actually an 'over-to-the-side, controller. This little panel provides all the data entry functions for the radios, weapons, sensors, and other systems that require programming. Next to it is the ejection seat controller, with three choices for exiting the aircraft. The NORM position will eject both crew, no matter who pulls the handle. SOLO will eject only the quitter, not the other crewman. AFT INITIATE means the 'wizzo' makes the call. Why all the choices? Well, more than one

perfectly good aircraft has been abandoned by an inexperienced passenger, and SOLO gives the aircraft commander a little consideration in the matter of quitting $44 million worth of taxpayers' money. AFT INITIATE, on the other hand, is for those low altitude situations where there isn't even time for the pilot to let go of the controls long enough to punch out. But if you get a ride in an F-15 the pilot will tell you to switch to SOLO — at least until he knows you very well.

The panel seems so simple and uncomplicated, but these four screens are the essence of the F-15 Strike Eagle's tremendous performance. Not only do they dispose of the traditional clutter and confusion of the cockpit, they permit

the weapons system officer to manage imagery, data, weapons status, target designations, flight control information, and communications with speed and efficiency under the most demanding of conditions.

The emblem of the 336th TFS 'Rocketeers' adorns the left conformal fuel tank just aft of the air intake.

The 334th TFS 'Eagles' was the last of the three units within the 4th Tactical Wing to transition from F-4E to F-15E.

(Right) The sleek surface of the aircraft is decorated here and there with little jewels: a radar warning antenna and navigation lights on the wingtip; and flat formation lights that glow green at night, when the nav lights and anti- collision strobe are off. The latter allows you to be invisible to the bad guys, but not so invisible that your wingman bumps into you.

The LANTIRN navigation pod hangs below the right intake.

The wing commander's jet taxies out for some evening ACM practice. This is the 'show' aircraft; when the wing gets tasked with a static display at an airshow, this is the jet that usually goes.

4: Things Under Wings

If you happened to be travelling across Iraq in a T-72 tank in January 1990, the odds are that one of these little devices ruined your whole day. Mate a standard Mk 84 HE 500 lb bomb with an electro-optical guidance seeker and trajectory-control fins, and this is what you get: a GBU-12B/B Paveway laser-guided bomb (LGB).

Practising a 'combat turn'. During wartime, aircraft must be quickly refuelled and rearmed after missions, then sent aloft again as quickly as the theatre commander requires. So the ground crews get out the stop watches and see how fast the bombs, missiles, bullets and tanks can get replaced. This is one of the most important events at the annual *Gunsmoke* competition, and one in which the pilot and 'wizzo' are merely spectators.

The seeker section is a strap-on device that can be attached to different iron bombs. During Gulf operations F-15Es carried up to eight of these weapons on the CFT rails, and they proved to be the ideal ordnance for tank-busting.

Mk 20 Rockeye II anti-armour cluster bomb. Inside the sheet metal case are hundreds of coffee-can sized bomblets. When the bomb is dropped a timer actuates a cord of explosive (visible on top of the case) that serves as a kind of can opener, dispensing the submunitions over an area that is typically about the size of a football field. The bomblets effectively saturate the area; if there are tanks or other armour in the target area (and there should be), the probability of one of the submunitions landing on each is high. And although the bomblets are small, they will easily blast a hole through the thin roof armour of any tank, spraying the interior with molten metal. Tanks subject to such treatment are normally flaming wrecks within about two seconds.

CBU-87 cluster bomb. This weapon is particularly effective against a wide variety of targets — troops, trucks, tanks, artillery, SAM sites, and the rest of the menu. It uses the same technology as the Mk 20 to dispense its submunitions.

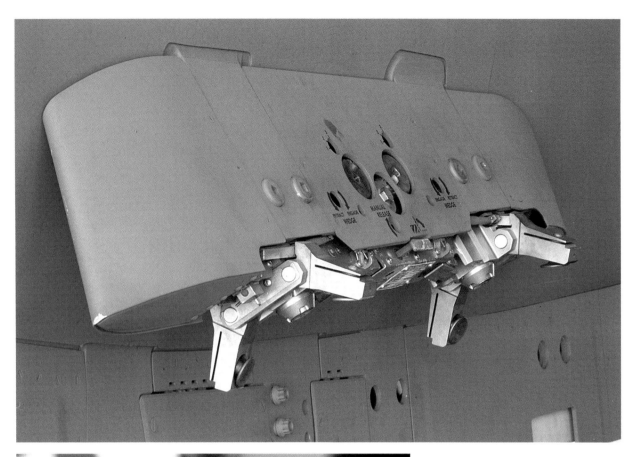

The bomb rack is attached to a conformal fuel tank. Latches within the rack assembly mate with fittings on the bombs; when released, the bombs are kicked off the aircraft in rapid sequence, as programmed by the 'wizzo'. Virtually any American bomb, including nukes and the 2,000 lb Mk 84, can be hung from these racks.

Mk 82 500 lb bomb with conventional fuse attached. The old, traditional 'pig iron' bombs may not be particularly accurate but they get many jobs done — and they're cheap! The fuse is activated first by the removal of the safety pin when the bomb comes off the rack, then by the wind-driven propeller which must spin for a while until the bomb is armed. This permits a safe getaway for the Strike Eagle from those oh-so-low deliveries.

Practising a 'combat turn'. The bombs are Mk 84 2,000 lb 'pig iron' munitions, often called 'dumb' bombs.

AF
88 1708

A full load of 500 lb Mk 82 'pig iron'.

CAPT MURRAY ROBE
LT AL HANSON

As *Desert Storm* fades into the history books, the mission markings are gradually being painted over. Some airframes flew a lot of missions, like this one; others flew very few. Three didn't come back at all, one being lost in a training accident before the war began, and two others being brought down by enemy action.

The well-dressed Eagle doesn't go anywhere without a missile or two. This one is an AIM-9 Sidewinder, a heat seeker. The design goes back to the 1950s, and is extremely simple and reliable. The old ones had to go up the adversary's tail pipe, but the new 'Limas' and 'Mikes' (as the L and M versions are called) are all-aspect missiles that will home on the friction-heated skin of the bad guy as easily as his exhaust. It is a true fire-and-forget missile, unlike the Sparrow, which relies on the launch aircraft's radar for continuous guidance all the way to the victim. The Sidewinder is used against close-in bogeys, the Sparrow against ones at longer range, out to about 60 miles. A newer air-to-air missile is the AMRAAM, a replacement for the Sparrow. It uses its own radar to track the target, making it a long range fire-and-forget weapon.

5: The Luke Connection

Before landing: master arm to SAFE, command mode to OFF, altimeters SET and CHECK, target FLIR to STBY/OFF, landing light ON, TF radar on or off as needed — and be sure the holding brake is OFF or you'll lose control after touchdown. Approach the pattern and the 'break', come back on the power to mantain pattern altitude and at least 300 knots airspeed, using the speed brake if necessary. Turn into the downwind leg, reduce power to slow below 250 knots; lower gear and flaps. Turn final, using small applications of power and angle of attack to maintain approach airspeed. As you flare the aircraft reduce power smoothly to IDLE; the wheels should return gently to the concrete.

They come to Luke from all over the Air Force's world: from Spangdahlem, Kadena, Turkey, and from all the bases in the continental US. They come from UPT and the introductory fighter pilot training programme at Holloman Air Force Base, New Mexico. They arrive with a few hours, young lieutenants and captains in their twenties; they come from long careers in Phantoms, F-111s, F-16s and F-15Cs, old majors and lieutenant-colonels in their forties. When Air Force fighter pilots and weapon systems operators talk about the 'schoolhouse solution' they're usually talking about Luke Air Force Base, the largest fighter aircrew training facility in the free world.

Luke is in the hot, dry Arizona desert 20 miles north-west of Phoenix. The base is home to two major schools, one for the single-seat F-16 Falcon, the other for the F-15, both C- and E- models. The F-15 programme is administered by the 405th Tactical Training Wing (TTW) and two component training squadrons, the 461st and the 550th.

The front-seaters already know how to fly an aeroplane when they arrive, and wear the 'radiator wings' of USAF pilots. The back-seaters have qualified as weapons systems officers, and they wear the 'spider-web' wings of a USAF 'wizzo'. But neither arrives knowing the F 15E Strike Eagle. Here is some of what they learn:

The F-15E Strike Eagle programme lasts a little over six months, and consists of both classwork and flying. The flying begins with a single-ship orientation flight,

Sprayed up with the 405th's traditional 'LA' tailcodes, this F-15E is in fact the second oldest Strike Eagle in service with the wing.

That red line isn't very wide or very bold, but try to think of it as an electrified fence surrounding the aircraft parking area. Step across it, however accidentally, and the Security Police will soon have you spread-eagled, your nose in the concrete and an M-16 aimed at your vital components.

(Right) The afterburner nozzle section of the Pratt & Whitney F1001 PW-220 engine expands and contracts to control the amount of thrust produced. In the process, the motors that drive all the little levers make a very strange howling noise audible at great distances.

an opportunity for the student to get acquainted with the $40 million plaything. The flight concentrates on one of the most important things you can do with an expensive jet — getting it back on the ground in one piece.

Then they'll get a couple of introductory formation flights, plus some experience with advanced handling manoeuvres. Much of the important part of a Strike Eagle's mission is spent in hard turns, at high G loads, inverted. The new Eagle drivers begin to see the world from an inverted position. All this is followed by more landings. Then come more advanced handling characteristics; like what happens when the heat is really turned up. They are slowly prepared for a set of techniques called 'basic fighter manoeuvres' — basic dog-fighting procedures. They get to wring the jet out from very fast to very slow, right up to its limits and sometimes beyond. The idea is to get the student comfortable and confident with stresses, strains, and perspectives that are very unusual.

Then come offensive and defensive basic fighter manoeuvres. The students get about eight rides, trying to get a shot on the instructor, then trying to deny the instructor's shot with guns and missiles. The air-to-air instruction gets the students thinking in three and four dimensions, gets them to anticipate and to position themselves in an adversary's 'six o'clock, position.

The instructors start gently, not pushing the novice fighter jocks very hard, watching how they react. 'If you start out well, I'm going to push up the level on you. I want to see if you were just lucky or can you think for yourself, make the moves, look over your shoulder and evaluate what I'm doing behind you. It is very difficult, but there are clues you can bring into your bag of tricks. You're not used to sustained Gs, but we do that here. That's what will get you the first time — it's a lot of hard work and you just can't give up. You get SO tired! You're huffing and puffing and the only thing you can do is to drop off the turn rate. When you do that it makes it a lot easier for me to get in there, solves a lot of problems for me to nail you. You have to learn to force what we call a 'closure problem'. I'm going to jam it in your face, and you've got to solve it or I'm going to reverse on you and get a shot. I'm not trying to beat you down physically, but beat you down mentally, to give you more problems than you can handle. When you make a bad move, I'm going to capitalize on it.'

The instructors will often say 'If you aren't cheating, you're not trying!' What they mean is, take maximum advantage of every opportunity. If an engagement is supposed to start at 420 knots, plus or minus 20, you should be looking at 440 knots calibrated airspeed on entry, most of the time. This provides the maximum amount of energy, and energy will usually make the difference. 'It means, don't put yourself in a worse situation than I give you. If I give you the opportunity to take an extra twenty knots — and twenty knots are worth having — then take it! '

Next comes advanced combat manoeuvring — the art of the two–ship formation. Now the pilots and EWOs get to fly lead and wing, learn to manage an attack and to support one. They are learning to work as

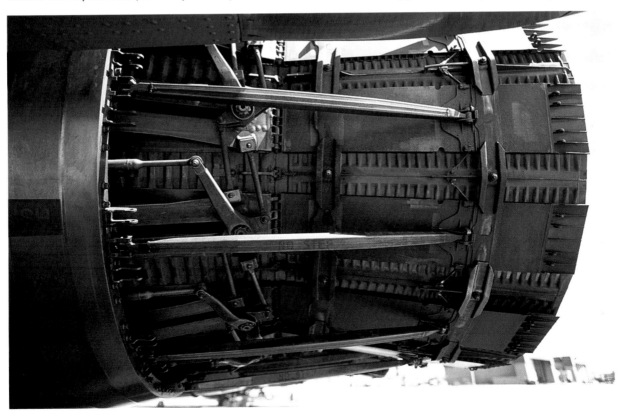

The 20 mm gun ammunition is loaded with this pneumatic system that attaches to the underside of the jet.

a team in the cockpit, and a team with the other aircraft. There are four ACM rides, two offensive, two defensive. They get a couple of 'intercept' rides where bogeys are picked up on radar at 40 miles, then chased and engaged — the foundation of the air-to-air mission. 'You start out 40 miles away from these two guys, and you have to figure out how to end up in a position of advantage on them. It is really choreographed — the two-ships have to talk to each other, make sure they've seen the bogey, make sure they have them on the radar, target them, employ good ordnance, merge, then try to pick up a 'tally two' as they come to the merge so they can convert on these guys if they didn't get a face-to-face kill initially', explains one of the instructors. And that's it for the air-to-air phase of the course!

But as good as the Strike Eagle may be against other aircraft, the meat of its mission is ground attack, and that's where most of the training rides and classroom work at Luke are focused. There are thousands of miles of desert surrounding Luke, and many ranges for bombing and gunnery. The students now learn the joys of dropping pig iron with precision. Typical flights involve low-level flight from Luke out to one of the ranges, then three or four kinds of deliveries. Instead of massive (and expensive) Mk 84 or other kinds of bombs, the students deliver tiny blue practice weapons that have the same trajectories as the real thing, but with only a small marking charge to show where they land. After a couple of introductory flights in daylight, the new Strike Eagle drivers and EWOs are introduced to LANTIRN, the night vision/targeting system. The system projects a clear image of the ground on the HUD, allowing the pilot to fly using visual cues on the darkest of nights, and to designate and engage targets, too. After a couple of flights under the hood, they start using LANTIRN at night.

They get acquainted with aerial refuelling, first during the day, later at night. They learn to deliver bombs at night, first in a low-threat environment, then in 'surface attack' mode — low-level tactical formations, defending against possible air-to-air threats, and using combat navigation tactics to approach the target area.

'It all culminates in their graduation ride. We take ten or twelve of them, give them live bombs, and run them up to a range, perhaps in Utah or down by Yuma, where we have some bogeys waiting to 'tap' them. That's the big excitement for these guys, their graduation exercise. They get to engage some targets, then go in and drop some real bombs, and come on back. Then they go off to a squadron.'

'They're awkward initially, they haven't seen any of this before. Guys will make mistakes — I expect that. It takes a year to get really comfortable in the jet, to know what's going on. That's about 200 or 250 hours. At that point you're a good wingman, and you start to learn about being flight lead. That's a lot harder, because it requires a lot more thinking in the air.'

Capt. John 'Zod' Mauer — an experienced 'wizzo'— has been flying RF-4s for a while, but they're leaving the inventory and he's going to stick around. He'll go to a new wing of Strike Eagles based at Elmendorf near Anchorage, Alaska.

(Right) Capt. Rick 'Bones' Dennee briefs two students before one of their early air-to-air rides. He will chase them around much of southern Arizona for an hour and a half. 'Goals for you out there today: 100 per cent sorting by ten nautical miles; defensive BFM — your best break turns; deny any and all shots I take on you today! Survive, or quickly go offensive and kill me. To survive, remember, get beyond 9,000 feet. Watch out for me intimidating you; remember the manoeuvres I've flown against you back there. If I've done a big turn around behind you, you know I was slow coming out of the turn, now I've gotta be slower still, so now you've gotta be ready to defeat the snap shot. Remember: you only use the vertical when you own the vertical — when I'm below your plane of motion and my nose is significantly down hill. Other keys: watch my 'stabs', work that into your cross check.'

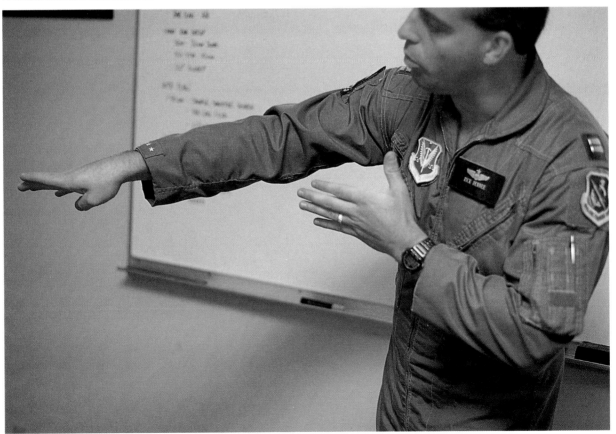

Concentrating on keeping his jet centred on the taxyway out to the blacktop, the trainee pilot in this 'clean' Strike Eagle has probably passed the pair of F-16s holding on an a joining taxy track without even seeing them. Both the Fighting Falcons belong to the similarly tasked 58th Tactical Training Wing, also based at Luke.

The emblem of the 461st Tactical Fighter Training Squadron is not, as you might expect, a picture of an instructor in a really bad mood, but a representation of the theatrical jester. The 461st goes back to 1956 when the squadron was formed at Landstuhl, Germany, and has been known since then as the 'Deadly Jesters'— after the rowdy antics of the young officers who were then flying F-86s and F-100s.

The 405th Tactical Fighter Training Wing is the schoolhouse for both the F-15C Eagle (single seat air-superiority) and the F-15E Strike Eagle (dual role, air-to-air and air-to-ground). About 800 students each year attend training at the school.

It gets so hot in Arizona that the jets need to wear these bras to keep their delicate parts from getting sunburnt.